The Really *Wild Life of Frogs*™

LEOPARD FROGS

DOUG WECHSLER

THE ACADEMY OF NATURAL SCIENCES

The Rosen Publishing Group's
PowerKids Press™
New York

For Bea, Barb, and Bama who introduced me to a new way of being in the outdoors

About the Author
Wildlife biologist, ornithologist, and photographer Doug Wechsler has studied birds, snakes, frogs, and other wildlife around the world. Doug Wechsler works at The Academy of Natural Sciences of Philadelphia, a natural history museum. As part of his job, he travels to rain forests and remote parts of the world to take pictures of birds. He has taken part in expeditions to Ecuador, the Philippines, Borneo, Cuba, Cameroon, and many other countries.

Published in 2002 by The Rosen Publishing Group, Inc.
29 East 21st Street, New York, NY 10010

First Edition

Book Design: Michael De Guzman, Emily Muschinske

Project Editor: Kathy Campbell

Photo Credits: All photos © Doug Wechsler.

Wechsler, Doug.
Leopard frogs / Doug Wechsler.
    p. cm. — (The really wild life of frogs)
Includes bibliographical references (p.   ).
  ISBN 0-8239-5856-6 (lib. bdg.)
1. Leopard frogs—Juvenile literature. [1. Leopard frogs. 2. Frogs.] I. Title.
  QL668.E27 W425 2002
  597.8'92—dc21
                                                                                            00–013207

Manufactured in the United States of America

CONTENTS

DOUG SAYS

LEOPARD FROGS CAN BE GREEN, BROWN, OR GRAY.

MINI-LEOPARDS

A creature with spots lurks in tall grass. It spies its **prey** and lunges. Quickly it swallows the prey whole.

You know this creature is not a leopard because leopards bite off chunks of food. Meet the leopard frog. You would hardly think that this is a dangerous creature, unless you were a grasshopper.

Leopard frogs are medium-size frogs that grow up to 5 inches (127 mm) long. There are eight **species** of leopard frogs in North America. A ninth species, the Vegas Valley leopard frog, is **extinct**. Small differences help you to tell the species apart, but most have rounded spots. Leopard frogs live in southern Canada, most of the United States, Mexico, and Central America.

LEOPARD FROG HOMES

Wetlands of many types are home to leopard frogs. Ponds, streams, and pools near rivers are good homes for them. All leopard frogs lay their eggs in water. Some southern leopard frogs **breed** in slightly salty waters near the Gulf Coast. Rio Grande leopard frogs often breed in the water tanks from which cattle drink. Lowland leopard frogs lay eggs in pools along creeks in the desert.

Leopard frogs do not live a lazy life, sitting on lily pads. During summer most leave the water and travel to meadows, bushy places, and open woods. There they can find plenty of insects to eat. Leopard frogs that live in dry climates cannot always wander very far away, but they still spend much of their time out of water.

A leopard frog that has hopped away from a body of water can absorb dew from the grass to stay moist.

DOUG SAYS

A FEW NORTHERN LEOPARD FROGS FROM THE MIDWESTERN UNITED STATES HAVE NO SPOTS.

LEOPARD SPOTS

Leopard frogs have spots like leopards. This is how they got their name. What good are spots? Both leopard frogs and leopards use spots for **camouflage**. Camouflage is an animal's natural disguise. Spots look like shadows. When a leopard frog or leopard is in a place with shadows, the spots make it hard to see the outline of the animal.

Try it yourself. Cut out two frogs on plain, brown paper. Draw dark spots on one and nothing on the other. Hide them in tall grass. Which one is easier to see? Leopard frogs and leopards use camouflage to escape their enemies and surprise their prey.

A southern leopard frog hides in the grass. Its spots make it harder to see.

Where do leopard frogs go in winter? As temperatures get close to freezing, leopard frogs swim to the bottom of a pond or stream. Leopard frogs spend the whole winter resting on the bottom. This is called **hibernation**. They do not take a single breath. They still need **oxygen**, but not much. Oxygen from the water seeps through their skin and moves into their blood. The frogs barely move all winter. Like all frogs, leopard frogs are cold-blooded. They do not need to warm their bodies from inside like we do.

When warm weather arrives at the end of winter, leopard frogs swim up to the surface. Soon they will join the choruses of wood frogs and **spring peepers**.

Leopard frogs are dark when they first come out of hibernation.

BREEDING SEASON

As winter ends, leopard frogs begin a chorus of chuckling grunts or **trills**. The ponds and streams where they live also come to life with noises of other frogs and toads. The frogs call to attract mates. Leopard frogs start to lay eggs as soon as winter ends. Some leopard frogs will lay eggs until summer. Southern leopard frogs may lay eggs at almost any time of year that is not near freezing.

A female leopard frog lays about 5,000 eggs at a time. She attaches the eggs to sticks or plants in the water. The eggs hatch in about 10 days. If the water is warm, they may hatch even faster. In cold water, hatching takes longer.

This southern leopard frog has filled its vocal sacs with air. The leopard frog's call for a mate can last from 2 to 3 seconds.

TADPOLES

When the egg hatches, a tiny tadpole wriggles out. It is about ⅓ inch (8 mm) long. At first the tadpole is not very active. Its mouth is still forming and it is not ready to eat. After a few days, the tadpole becomes active and spends most of its time eating. Over the next two months, the tadpole grows quickly. As it reaches full size, its hind legs and toes start to grow. About the time all five toes appear, its arms start to pop through its sides. Big changes also take place inside the tadpole. Its lungs grow. It no longer breathes through the **gills**. Its mouth and eyes get bigger. Its gut shortens. It stops eating only plants and starts eating only animals. The change from tadpole to frog is called **metamorphosis**.

A few days after the tadpole's arms first begin to grow out of its body, the tadpole becomes a frog.

Northern leopard frogs are about 1 inch (25 mm) long at metamorphosis. The young frogs usually stay near the shore at first. As they get older, they move into meadows and open woods. Tall grasses are safe places for frogs to hide. Meadows are also full of insects that leopard frogs like to eat. The young frogs fatten up quickly. By autumn they are almost twice as long as when they left the water.

By the following summer, the frogs are usually more than 2 ½ inches (64 mm) long. In cold climates, leopard frogs grow more slowly. In northern Michigan, it can take up to four years before they become adults and breed.

It is fall. This fat, female, southern leopard frog is full of eggs. She will lay the eggs in spring.

LEOPARD FROG EATERS

Leopard frogs are good to eat. Just ask a bullfrog, a garter snake, or a red-shouldered hawk. In the South, where leopard frogs grow large, people also hunt them for their legs.

From the time a leopard frog starts out as an egg, it is in danger. Fish, bullfrog tadpoles, and **newts** eat frog eggs. The jelly around the eggs protects them from some enemies. Once they hatch, dragonfly **nymphs**, **back swimmers**, and **water tigers** join the feast. Water tigers are young water beetles, and back swimmers are bugs that swim upside down. Frogs that have just metamorphosed are a little slow. Green herons, raccoons, and other **predators** gobble them up.

A green heron eats a large leopard frog tadpole.
Dragonfly nymphs eat smaller tadpoles.

LEOPARD FROG MENUS

Leopard frogs eat more different kinds of foods than you find on a restaurant menu. Beetles, flies, grasshoppers, worms, mayflies, dragonflies, moths, butterflies, caterpillars, and small frogs are part of a leopard frog's diet.

When a leopard frog spies a moving beetle nearby, it lunges forward. At the same time, it opens its mouth. Out shoots its tongue. The sticky tongue traps the insect and brings it back to the mouth.

Once the food is in its mouth, the frog swallows it whole. As it swallows, it pushes its eyes inward. The backs of the eyes push on the roof of the mouth. This helps to send the yummy beetle down the frog's throat.

The leopard frog takes from two to three years to grow to adult size. It can live up to nine years.

FROGS IN TROUBLE

Humans have changed the **environment** in many ways that have harmed leopard frogs. We have filled many of their wetlands. We have accidentally carried diseases from one pond to another. We have polluted the air and the water.

One species of leopard frog became extinct when the city of Las Vegas grew and destroyed the frog's habitat. The streams and springs that were home to leopard frogs were covered with pavement or were dried up.

In some places, leopard frogs have disappeared. In others they are rare. In many other places they are still very common. We can help leopard frogs by being more careful about how we treat our environment.

GLOSSARY

back swimmers (BAK SWIM-mers) Bugs that live in water and swim upside down.

breed (BREED) To get together in order to mate and lay eggs or have babies.

camouflage (KA-muh-flahj) The color or pattern of an animal's feathers, fur, or skin that helps it blend into its surroundings.

environment (en-VY-urn-ment) All living things and conditions that make up a place.

extinct (ik-STINKT) No longer existing.

gills (GILS) An organ in certain water animals that takes oxygen out of the water.

hibernation (hy-bur-NAY-shun) Spending the winter sleeping or resting.

metamorphosis (meh-tuh-MOR-fuh-sis) A complete change in form. For example, a tadpole changes to a frog.

newts (NOOTS) Small, brightly colored salamanders that live in or around water.

nymphs (NIMFS) Young insects that have not yet developed into adults.

oxygen (AHK-sih-jin) A gas in the air that has no color, taste, or odor and is necessary for people and animals to breathe.

predators (PREH-duh-terz) Animals that kill other animals for food.

prey (PRAY) An animal that is eaten by another animal for food.

species (SPEE-sheez) A single kind of plant or animal. For example, all people are one species.

spring peepers (SPRING PEEP-urz) Small brown treefrogs that make a high, sharp sound.

trills (TRILZ) Rapidly repeating musical notes.

water tigers (WAH-tur TY-gurz) The young of diving beetles.

wetlands (WET-lands) Land, other than streams, lakes, and open ocean, that is covered by water. Marshes, swamps, and bogs are some types of wetlands.

INDEX

B
beetles, 21
breed(ing), 6, 13, 17
butterflies, 21

C
camouflage, 9
caterpillars, 21
cold-blooded, 10

D
dragonflies, 21

E
egg(s), 6, 13, 14, 18
enemies, 9, 18
extinct, 5, 22

F
flies, 21
food, 5, 6, 17, 21

G
gills, 14
grasshoppers, 21

H
hibernation, 10

M
mayflies, 21
metamorphosis, 14, 17
moths, 21

P
predators, 18
prey, 5, 9

S
species, 5, 22

T
tadpole, 14
trills, 13

W
weather, 10
wetlands, 6, 22
winter, 10, 13
worms, 21

WEB SITES

To learn more about leopard frogs, check out these Web sites:

www.cmnh.org/research/vertzoo/frogs/pipiens.html

www.gov.ab.ca/env/fw/threatsp/frog/sta.html

www.herpnet.net/Iowa-Herpetology/amphibians/frogs_toads/plainsleopard.html

www.npwrc.usgs.gov/narcam/idguide/ranaut.htm